SEE AMERICA

THE REVOLUTIONARY WAR

1775–1783

★

The Art of

MORT KÜNSTLER

Text by

ALAN AXELROD

★

ABBEVILLE KIDS

A DIVISION OF ABBEVILLE PRESS

New York   London

Especially for my grandchildren,
Andrew, Laura, and Tom.

Front and back cover: The Declaration of Independence is read to the troops. See page 16.
Frontispiece: Washington arrives at Valley Forge. See page 20.
Back endpaper: Cornwallis surrenders at Yorktown. See page 34.

Editor: Nicole Lanctot
Designer: Misha Beletsky
Composition: Ada Rodriguez
Production manager: Louise Kurtz

First edition
1 3 5 7 9 10 8 6 4 2

ISBN 978-0-7892-1253-5

For bulk or premium sales and for text adoption procedures, write to Customer Service Manager, 116 West 23rd Street, New York, NY 10011, or call 1-800-Artbook.
Visit Abbeville Press online at www.abbeville.com.

TABLE OF CONTENTS

The Story of the Revolutionary War

In 1607, a group of English men and women sailed across the Atlantic Ocean to start a colony in North America. They set up a little village in Virginia and called it Jamestown to honor their king back in England, James I.

The colony started out with just 144 people. But, during a winter much harsher than any they had known in the Old World, half died from sickness or starvation. With the help of their Native American neighbors, the others survived, and the colony grew. By 1732, thirteen English colonies were set up in North America, and we know them today as states: Virginia, New York, Massachusetts, Maryland, Rhode Island, Connecticut, New Hampshire, Delaware, North Carolina, South Carolina, New Jersey, Pennsylvania, and Georgia.

Most of the people in the colonies had been born in Britain, or their parents or grandparents were born there. In these new colonies, they believed they were equal to any English man or woman who still lived in Britain.

In 1764, the English Parliament and King George III said that the colonists must start paying taxes to England, though they did not have a voice in its government. Many colonists believed that "taxation without representation" would be unfair, and they decided not to pay taxes. Some talked about fighting against the king. So King George III sent armed soldiers to the American colonies. They were known as Redcoats, because of their scarlet uniforms. The soldiers only made things worse. On March 5, 1770, a fight broke out between some Redcoats and some citizens of Boston. Six citizens died. It was called "The Boston Massacre."

Many thought a revolution would now begin, but King George III and Parliament finally agreed to end all of the taxes on the colonies—except the tax on tea. To protest the tea tax, 150 colonists who called themselves the Sons of Liberty boarded three tea ships in Boston Harbor on December 16, 1773.

They threw 342 crates of tea into the water. This "Boston Tea Party" made the king and Parliament very angry. They punished Boston by passing harsh laws and sending more Redcoats.

Redcoats marched from Boston to Concord, Massachusetts, to seize guns and ammunition from the colonists. Some colonists had promised to be ready to fight at a minute's notice. These "Minutemen" now fought the Redcoats at Lexington and Concord on April 19, 1775, stopping the Redcoats from taking guns and ammunition. These two fights were the first battles of the Revolutionary War.

The colonists had already formed an American version of Parliament. They called it the "Continental Congress." This Continental Congress now called for the formation of a "Continental Army." A wealthy Virginia farmer and military officer, George Washington, was chosen to lead the colonial soldiers.

While the Continental Army fought the Redcoats as well as other colonists who wanted to remain loyal to the king, the members of the Continental Congress signed a Declaration of Independence on July 4, 1776. It announced to the world the birth of a new nation, the United States.

The Declaration of Independence said that everyone is "created equal." For this reason, the Continental Congress decided to separate from Britain.

At first, the Revolution went well for Washington's soldiers, but Great Britain was the mightiest empire of its time. It had a big army and navy.

By December 1776, many people thought the United States had lost the Revolution. But, on Christmas night, Washington led part of his army across the Delaware River from Pennsylvania to New Jersey (LEFT). On the morning of December 26, he attacked a camp of Hessians (German soldiers hired to fight for the British) in Trenton, New Jersey. His troops were victorious, and the Revolution gained new energy.

The Americans, however, still suffered many more defeats. Even with France's help, the war continued to be a hard struggle. After surviving a cruel winter at Valley Forge, Pennsylvania, in late 1777 and early 1778, the Continental Army continued to fight. The British captured Savannah (in Georgia) and Charleston (in South Carolina), but American generals also won important battles.

Then came fall 1781. Washington's Continental Army was joined by a French army led by the French general Comte de Rochambeau. Together, they trapped a large British army commanded by General Charles Cornwallis at Yorktown, Virginia. The surrender of Cornwallis on October 19, 1781, ended most of the fighting. Two years later, on September 3, 1783, the two sides signed the Treaty of Paris, which officially ended the war and recognized American independence. The colonists had won, and the Revolution was over!

The First Colonists and the Boston Massacre

★1770

The English men and women who started colonies in America faced many dangers. The first colonists crossed thousands of miles of ocean in wooden sailing ships. They grew or raised all their own food.

This painting shows a proud and peaceful farm family. But many new colonists became angry because they had to pay taxes to England, even though no one in its government was looking out for them.

In Britain, lawmakers in Parliament represented the people. American colonists had no representatives in Parliament. When they complained about this and did not pay taxes, King George III sent soldiers to force them to obey him and to pay. How do you think the colonists felt?

On March 5, 1770, in Boston, Massachusetts, angry people threatened a British soldier on guard duty. When other soldiers came to help him, the people threw bricks, snowballs, and ice at them. Some soldiers fired muskets. One of six people that the British killed was a man named Crispus Attucks, who was believed to be an escaped slave. We see him on the far left, in the snow.

Word of this "Boston Massacre" spread, and colonists began to think about going to war to free themselves from their king.

The Boston Tea Party

★1773

Hoping to calm the heated feelings, Parliament ended all of the taxes except for a tax on the drink the colonists liked best: tea.

Sam Adams was the leader of a group called the Sons of Liberty. To protest the tea tax, he organized a very special "tea party."

Three tea ships were anchored in Boston Harbor. On the night of December 16, 1773, one hundred fifty Sons of Liberty, disguised as Mohawk Indians to hide their true identities, made their way to Griffin's Wharf. The Sons of Liberty divided into three groups of fifty men. They took rowboats out to the ships, climbed aboard, and threw a total of 342 crates of tea into the water. Look closely at the picture on the far right. Each crate—called a "chest"—was packed with tea. Throwing them overboard was hard work!

To punish Boston for this "tea party," Parliament passed laws closing the port of Boston to damage business in the city. Parliament also took away many of the colonists' rights and sent more soldiers into Boston. The colonists got ready for war.

The soldiers (RIGHT) were called "Redcoats." Can you tell why?

Liberty or Death

★1775

Patrick Henry was a member of the House of Burgesses, where Virginia's elected representatives gathered to lead their colony. Henry told the other lawmakers that Virginia had the right to govern itself, without asking permission from the British Parliament. Lord Dunmore was the man King George III had sent to govern Virginia. Angered by Henry's talk, he shut down the House of Burgesses.

The lawmakers found other places to meet. On March 23, 1775, they gathered at St. John's Episcopal Church in Richmond, Virginia. That day, Henry stood up to make his most important speech. He said Virginia should join with Massachusetts and other colonies to fight the king and Parliament. It was a choice between slavery to Britain and war, he said.

"I know not what course others may take, but as for me, give me liberty or give me death!" he declared. These words convinced Virginia's leaders to recruit soldiers for a war to free the colonies from Britain.

This cannon (RIGHT) used in the Revolutionary War was made of brass. Cannons were mounted on sturdy wooden "carriages" with big wheels. Horses pulled them into battle.

Paul Revere and the Battles of Lexington and Concord

★1775

King George III chose General Thomas Gage as the military governor of Massachusetts. On April 18, 1775, General Gage ordered about 700 Redcoats to march 20 miles from Boston to Concord, Massachusetts. He told them to seize weapons that the colonists stored there.

Paul Revere was a Patriot, as American freedom fighters were called. He knew the Redcoats were up to something, but wasn't sure what. So he sent his friend John Pulling to the steeple of Old North Church in Boston. If Pulling saw Redcoats marching out of the city by land, he would shine a single lantern from the steeple. If he saw them board boats to take them across the Back Bay, he would shine two lanterns: "One if by land, two if by sea." See the lights? (ABOVE)

When Revere saw two lanterns in the steeple, he knew the Redcoats were going across the bay, headed to Concord. With two other Patriots, Williams Dawes and Samuel Prescott, he galloped all night, shouting a warning to wake up the Minutemen. They were volunteers who promised to be ready for battle on a minute's notice. Most people believe Revere cried out, "The British are coming!" but he actually shouted, "The regulars are out!" "Regulars," meaning the "regular" standing army, was another word for the Redcoats.

At sunrise on April 19, 1775, some of the Minutemen fought the Redcoats at Lexington, on the road to Concord. Later, at Concord, more Minutemen waited near the North Bridge over the Concord River. They fired on the Redcoats, forcing them to return to Boston. The Battles of Lexington and Concord were the first battles of the Revolution.

The Declaration of Independence

★1776

At the start of the Revolutionary War, the colonists were divided. Half of them wanted to become a new country. Half wanted to stay loyal to King George III. This second group of people were called

"Tories," or "Loyalists." Many wore red uniforms (RIGHT) and fought against the Patriots, who wore blue.

Patriot leaders asked Thomas Jefferson to write a "Declaration of Independence" to explain to the whole world why America needed to be free.

"We hold these truths to be self-evident," Jefferson wrote, "that all men are created equal" and that everyone has the right to "Life, Liberty and the pursuit of Happiness." He also wrote that if a government fails to support equality of its people and these rights, the people should throw out that government and create a better one.

Representatives from all the American colonies met in Philadelphia as the Continental Congress (BELOW). On July 4, 1776, they voted to approve the Declaration of Independence.

On that day, the United States was born. Patriot commanders read copies of the declaration to their soldiers, as seen on the left page. Those soldiers were called "Bluecoats," even though the new country could not afford to buy uniforms for all of them.

Washington Crosses the Delaware
★1776

George Washington commanded the American army, called the Continental Army. During the summer and fall of 1776, the Redcoats defeated the Continental Army in New York and then chased it across New Jersey and into Pennsylvania.

Many people, including the top British commander, General William Howe, believed Washington would give up. They thought the American Revolution had been crushed, and crushed quickly. But Washington soon proved them wrong.

On Christmas night, Washington loaded 2,400 soldiers and eighteen cannons onto flat ferryboats, like those in the painting (LEFT). They crossed the icy Delaware River from Pennsylvania to New Jersey. In freezing rain and dark, Washington and his men silently marched nine miles to Trenton to attack a camp of Hessians. The Hessians were German soldiers who wore tall "grenadier" hats and blue coats trimmed in gold (RIGHT). The British paid them to join the fight against the Patriots.

Washington and his men surprised the camp on the morning after Christmas. The Hessian soldiers were sleepy from celebrating. After less than two hours of fighting, they gave up. The Continental Army had just beaten the best soldiers in Europe. The Revolutionary War would go on!

Valley Forge Winter
★1777–1778

Have you ever been cold and hungry? During the whole winter of 1777 to 1778, General Washington's Continental Army was very cold and very hungry.

At the time of the Revolution, armies did not usually fight during the winter. They went into "winter quarters" to wait for warmer "fighting weather." The Continental Army waited at Valley Forge, Pennsylvania. But the new United States could barely afford to feed, clothe, and shelter its army.

This painting shows Washington on his horse, Nelson. The man facing Washington and Nelson is General Friedrich von Steuben. He came all the way from Germany to help the Americans fight for independence. He helped Washington to train the army. Thanks to him, soon Washington's group became as good as the best armies in Europe. The Continental Army survived the winter. By spring, it had learned much from General von Steuben and was stronger and smarter than ever before.

Washington and the Giant Chain

★1778

George Washington had found out that the British planned to sail up the Hudson River from New York City to attack New England.

He decided to prevent this by building a strong fort overlooking the river at West Point. He also hired a nearby ironworks to forge a gigantic iron chain, 1,500 feet long, made up of 750 links. Each link was two to three feet long and weighed more than one hundred pounds. This great chain stretched across the Hudson River from

West Point to Constitution Island. It was strong enough to stop large boats from moving past the guns of West Point. Each winter, it had to be pulled in before the river froze. Here, General Washington uses a telescope to observe the work.

About 9,000 African Americans fought on the Patriot side in the Revolution. Black slaves who joined the 1st Rhode Island Regiment (ABOVE) were set free after the war.

"I Have Not Yet Begun to Fight!"

★1779

The British Royal Navy went to war with 270 mighty warships, while the United States had no warships at all. The colonies bought and built a few ships as fast as they could. But who would command them?

John Paul Jones came to North America from Scotland shortly before the Revolution. When fighting began, he joined the new Continental Navy. He was so skilled as a sailor that he was given command of his own ship. Jones named it USS *Bonhomme Richard*.

On September 23, 1779, *Bonhomme Richard* fought a nighttime battle against a much bigger British warship, HMS *Serapis*.

Early in the fight, two of Captain Jones's biggest guns exploded. In this painting, which ship do you think is Jones's *Bonhomme Richard*? Can you see the flames through his boat's gun ports and windows?

After the explosion, Captain Jones purposely rammed the *Serapis*. The British captain thought that Jones had lost control of his ship. The captain called out to ask if Jones was giving up.

"I have not yet begun to fight!" Jones shouted back.

The two ships then drew apart and crashed together again. Captain Jones ordered his men to tie *Bonhomme Richard* to *Serapis*. See the ropes connecting the two ships? He then fired his cannons over and over. After two hours of this, the *Serapis* surrendered.

Because Captain Jones never gave up, Britain no longer ruled the world's oceans!

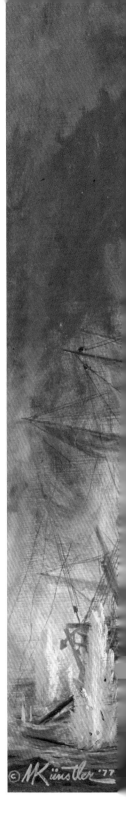

Spies

★1780

Some Patriots volunteered to spy for General Washington. The most famous was Nathan Hale, a Connecticut schoolteacher. After the British caught him and were about to hang him, he spoke these words: "I only regret that I have but one life to give for my country." He was just 21 years old.

After Hale was killed, Washington ordered an officer named Benjamin Tallmadge to recruit more spies. In 1780, Tallmadge's "Culper Spy Ring" uncovered British plans to ambush the whole French army when it arrived in Rhode Island. The spy in this picture (LEFT) is using a magnifying glass to read a warning message written in code.

Hale was the most famous spy of the Revolutionary War, but women and children were some of the best. No one suspected them. Many children volunteered. Spying was dangerous work. On July 7, 1779, 2,000 Redcoats and Hessians raided Fairfield, Connecticut, and set it on fire. Do the colors of this painting (RIGHT) make you feel the heat of the flames? Anyone caught spying was captured and threatened with death, no matter how young.

Lafayette Brings Great News

★1780

The Marquis de Lafayette, a young French nobleman, believed in liberty and equality. He crossed the Atlantic Ocean to serve as an officer in the Continental Army. Although he was just twenty years old, the Continental Congress made him a major general.

After fighting bravely, Lafayette returned to France during the winter of 1779–1780. He came back to North America in the spring of 1780. This painting shows Washington (hands behind his back) and Lafayette (next to him). They are listening to an officer read to the soldiers the great news Lafayette brought from France: King Louis XVI was sending a French army and a fleet of French warships to help the American colonists win their independence!

Look at the three boys closest to the cannon. Young boys served in the Continental Army as drummers and as artillery helpers. They carried gunpowder and cannonballs to the guns. They also fetched buckets of water to cool the cannon barrel so that it could be safely reloaded.

Everybody Made Sacrifices

★1781

A plantation house in South Carolina has been taken over by 175 British soldiers. The British flag (called the Union Jack) flies outside of it. Can you spot it? Two American commanders, Francis Marion (called "The Swamp Fox") and "Light Horse Harry" Lee, talk to the owner of the house, Mrs. Motte, who is glad they are there. They tell her they are forcing out the British by shooting flaming arrows to set the house on fire. Some American soldiers shoot at Redcoats trying to put out the fires burning on the house's roof.

Lee puts his hand gently on Mrs. Motte's shoulder to comfort her. Mrs. Motte is a Patriot. She says she is happy to sacrifice her house for the good of the country. Meanwhile, "The Swamp Fox" gives instructions to the men preparing the arrows.

This story will end happily. The Redcoats will surrender before the house is burned down, and Mrs. Motte will treat both sides to a delicious dinner.

In both the British and American armies during the Revolution, fifes and drums were played to make marching easier (LEFT). The instruments were also used to signal alerts and orders.

The Siege of Yorktown

★1781

On September 28, 1781, General Washington and the Comte de Rochambeau, commander of the French army, began an attack on the British army of General Charles Cornwallis at Yorktown, Virginia.

After pounding Cornwallis's army for a week with cannon fire, General Washington personally began digging the first of several trenches to use as cover to bring the cannons even closer to the enemy. In this painting (RIGHT) a Patriot points out an enemy position to his comanding officer.

After his men dug for three days, General Washington lit the fuse to fire the first shot in the Siege of Yorktown.

One of Rochambeau's soldiers (BELOW) poses against the flag of his regiment, which was called "Le Soissonnais" because its members came from the town of Soissons in France.

Victory at Yorktown!

★1781

For nearly a month, the armies of Generals Washington and Rochambeau fought the British army of General Charles Cornwallis at Yorktown. At last, on October 19, the British commander was ready to surrender.

The French and American armies lined up. This painting shows the French army on the right side of the road and the American army on the left side. The two lines were one mile long. Washington, mounted on his horse and beside his blue-coated Patriots, stood in the American line.

Lord Cornwallis said he was too sick to surrender in person and sent another officer in his place. As the British band played a tune called "The World Turned Upside Down," Brigadier General Charles O'Hara offered Cornwallis's sword to Rochambeau. The French general said nothing. He just shook his head "no" and pointed to General Washington. But when O'Hara tried to present the sword to him, Washington also shook his head. He pointed to General Benjamin Lincoln, who rode forward on his horse to accept the sword, pictured here. Back in May 1780, Lincoln had been forced to surrender *his* sword, to the British after they captured Charleston.

Seven thousand Redcoats marched off to prison camps that day—the day the United States earned the right to be called a nation.

Washington Rescues the Revolution

★1783

The victory at Yorktown in 1781 ended most of the fighting in the Revolutionary War. The United States and Great Britain did not sign an official treaty until 1783. During that time, the Continental Army nearly turned against the Continental Congress!

The long war had been so costly that there was no money to pay the soldiers. Their families were struggling to survive. Angry Continental Army officers called on General Washington to lead them in rebellion against the country they had just fought to create.

George Washington met with his officers in Newburgh, New York. He could have led them against the Continental Congress. He could have become America's dictator or even king. Instead, he calmly asked his officers to trust Congress. He then took a letter from his pocket. It explained the problems Congress was having raising money to pay the troops.

Before starting to read it, he put on eyeglasses. Washington's men had never seen him in glasses (LEFT).

"Gentlemen, you must pardon me," he said. "I have grown gray in your service and now find myself growing blind."

Washington's officers voted to stop talking about rebellion. They had so much faith in Washington that they decided to trust the Continental Congress because Washington trusted it. The new American nation was saved.

By 1783, George Washington was fifty-one years old. Like many middle-aged people, he needed glasses for reading, but his long-distance vision remained sharp as ever (ABOVE).

Washington's Homecoming

★1783

After the Revolution was won, the people were very grateful to George Washington. They called him "the father of his country."

Washington did not seek power or any other reward from the nation he helped to create. For this, even King George III called him "the greatest man in the world."

After saying good-bye to his army, Washington headed to Mount Vernon, his beloved home in Virginia. He arrived on Christmas Eve 1783, and he kissed and hugged his wife, Martha. In this painting on the left, the night appears very cold, but the house looks so warm!

After eight years of war, Washington wanted to live quietly. Six years later, however, he answered his nation's call again to become its first president.

★ The Revolutionary War: Timeline

1764–1769
Parliament passes laws taxing the American colonies.

1765
March 22: The Stamp Act requires most printed materials made in the colonies to be produced on special stamped paper purchased from the British government. It is Parliament's first serious attempt to force colonial obedience to Britain.

March 24: The Quartering Act of 1765 requires colonies to house and feed British soldiers.

October 7 and 25: The "Stamp Act Congress" brings together in New York City representatives from several colonies to decide how to protest the Stamp Act.

1767
June 29: The Townshend Revenue Act taxes glass, oil, lead, paper, and tea.

1768
August 1: Boston responds to the Townshend taxes with a Non-Importation Agreement. Boston merchants and traders stop importing taxed goods from Britain.

1770
Responding to colonists' protests, especially the Non-Importation Agreement, Parliament repeals all taxes, except for the tax on tea.

March 5: The Boston Massacre takes place. It is a street fight between a "Patriot" mob — throwing snowballs, ice, stones, and sticks — and a squad of Redcoats. The Redcoats fire on the Patriots, killing six people. Local leaders use the event to try to stir up a revolution.

1773
December 16: The Boston Tea Party protests the tea tax. At night, members of the Sons of Liberty storm three cargo ships in Boston Harbor and hurl 342 chests of tea into the water — before the taxes are paid on them. They disguise themselves as Mohawk Indians so that authorities cannot identify them.

1774
March 31–June 22: Parliament passes the harsh "Intolerable Acts" as punishment for the Boston Tea Party. These include laws closing the port of Boston, limiting colonial authority, and increasing the number of Redcoats quartered in Boston.

September 5–October 26: Passage of the "Intolerable Acts" prompts the First Continental Congress to meet in Philadelphia to discuss a united response to the British government, including the possibility of revolution.

1775

March 23: Virginia lawyer and member of the House of Burgesses Patrick Henry urges Virginia to unite with Massachusetts and other colonies in a revolt against Britain. "I know not what course others may take," he says, "but as for me, give me liberty or give me death!"

April 18: Paul Revere (along with William Dawes and Samuel Prescott) makes a "Midnight Ride" to alert the Minutemen that the Redcoats are on the march.

April 19: The Revolutionary War begins with the Battles of Lexington and Concord.

May 10: Patriots capture Fort Ticonderoga, New York.

June 10 and 15: The Continental Congress creates the Continental Army and appoints George Washington to lead it.

June 17: The Battle of Bunker Hill is fought (mostly on nearby Breed's Hill) in Charlestown, Massachusetts. The British drive the Americans off the hill, but suffer very heavy casualties.

1776

January 9: Thomas Paine, a recent immigrant to America, publishes *Common Sense*, promoting the idea of independence.

March 17: Surrounded by Patriot forces, the British army flees Boston for Canada.

July 4: The Continental Congress declares independence. The United States is born.

August 27: Redcoats defeat Washington in the Battle of Long Island (New York); the Continental Army retreats to New York City.

September 15: The British occupy New York City.

September 16: Washington holds his ground at the Battle of Harlem Heights before retreating to White Plains, New York.

October 28: Washington loses the Battle of White Plains and begins a long retreat through New Jersey and into Pennsylvania. Many believe the Revolution is already lost.

December 25–26: Washington crosses the Delaware River from Pennsylvania to New Jersey with a portion of the Continental Army. He marches to Trenton, where he defeats Hessian forces at the Battle of Trenton. The Revolution is given new life.

1777

January 3: Washington wins the Battle of Princeton.

January 6–May 28: Washington and the Continental Army go into winter quarters at Morristown, New Jersey.

July 27: The Marquis de Lafayette arrives in Philadelphia from France to offer his services in the American Revolution.

September 11: The British win the Battle of Brandywine, Pennsylvania, forcing Washington to retreat to Philadelphia, at the time the United States capital.

September 26: The British capture Philadelphia. In advance of the battle, the Continental Congress flees first to Lancaster and then to York, Pennsylvania.

October 4: Washington unsuccessfully attacks Germantown, five miles north of British-held Philadelphia.

October 7: Americans win the Battle of Saratoga, New York.

October 17: Defeated at Saratoga, British general John Burgoyne surrenders his army to American forces. The American victory convinces France to increase its aid to the Patriots.

1777–1778

In the so-called Conway Cabal, a group of Continental Army officers, including Brigadier General Thomas Conway, conspire to have George Washington replaced as commander in chief. They fail.

1778

April 30: Washington orders a great chain to be laid across the Hudson River at West Point to block passage of British ships.

May 4: The United States and France sign a Treaty of Alliance against Great Britain.

June 18: The British abandon Philadelphia and return to New York.

June 19: After a hard winter encamped at Valley Forge, Pennsylvania, the Continental Army resumes the fight.

June 28: The Battle of Monmouth Court House, New Jersey, ends in a draw.

December 29: Savannah, Georgia, falls to the British.

1779

February 23–24: American frontier general George Rogers Clark captures Vincennes (in present-day Indiana) on the Wabash River. It is an important Patriot victory on the western frontier of the colonies.

July 7: To punish Fairfield, Connecticut, for spying and other acts of resistance, British troops set fire to the town.

July 11: In a British raid, houses and shops in Norwalk, Connecticut, are burned.

July 15–16: The dashing American general "Mad Anthony" Wayne captures Stony Point, New York.

August 19: Another brilliant American general, "Light Horse Harry" Lee, attacks Paulus Hook, New Jersey.

September 23: USS *Bonhomme Richard* (John Paul Jones, captain) captures HMS *Serapis*. It is the greatest naval victory of the Revolutionary War.

1780

May 12: Charleston, South Carolina, falls to the British.

May 19: British and Loyalist forces led by Banastre Tarleton crush American troops at Waxhaws Creek, South Carolina.

July 11: A French army lands at Newport, Rhode Island, ready to aid the Americans.

August 16: Camden, South Carolina, falls to the British.

September 23: Americans capture British major John André, which leads to the exposure of Patriot general Benedict Arnold as a traitor who planned to turn over West Point to the British.

October 7: Americans win the Battle of Kings Mountain, South Carolina, near the border with North Carolina.

1781

January 1: Troops of the Pennsylvania Line mutiny to protest terrible conditions, lack of supplies, and failure to be paid. The mutiny is settled on January 8.

January 17: Americans win the Battle of Cowpens, South Carolina.

March 2: The Continental Congress adopts the Articles of Confederation, which serve as the first constitution of the United States.

March 15: The British win the Battle of Guilford Court House (North Carolina), but at great cost.

October 19: Lord Cornwallis surrenders to Washington and Rochambeau at Yorktown, Virginia. It is the last major battle of the Revolutionary War.

1782

July 11: British leave Savannah, Georgia.

November 30: British and Americans sign preliminary Articles of Peace.

December 14: British leave Charleston, South Carolina.

1783

September 3: United States and Britain sign the Treaty of Paris. Britain recognizes American independence. The American Revolution is officially over.

November 25: British troops leave New York City.

December 23: His mission accomplished, George Washington resigns as commander in chief of the Continental Army.

1787

September 17: The United States Constitution is signed.

1788

June 21: After New Hampshire ratifies the Constitution, it replaces the Articles of Confederation as the foundation of United States law.

★ The Revolutionary War: Key People

Adams, John (1735–1826) · An organizer of the Revolutionary War, Adams was one of the negotiators of the Treaty of Paris that ended the war in 1783. He was the new nation's first vice president (under George Washington) and its second president.

Adams, Samuel (1722–1803) · A fiery orator, Adams (second cousin of John Adams) was an organizer of the Massachusetts and national independence movements. He was a founder and leader of the Sons of Liberty.

Attucks, Crispus (c. 1723–1770) · Believed to be a runaway slave, Attucks was shot by the British during the Boston Massacre, and his death is considered the first casualty in the American fight for independence.

Brant, Joseph (1742–1807) · This Mohawk political and military leader was Britain's most skillful and effective Indian ally against the Patriots.

Burgoyne, John ("Gentleman Johnny") (1722–1792) · American general Horatio Gates defeated this British general at Bemis Heights in the Battle of Saratoga (1777).

Cornwallis, Charles (1738–1805) · This British general was defeated by Generals Washington and Rochambeau at the Battle of Yorktown (1781), the last major fight in the Revolution.

Franklin, Benjamin (1706–1790) · A philosopher, printer, author, and inventor, Franklin helped to organize the Revolutionary War, helped to secure an alliance with France, and was one of the principal negotiators of the Treaty of Paris (1783).

Gage, Thomas (1719 or 1720–1787) · Gage was the military governor of Massachusetts whose attempt to seize colonial arms at Concord, Massachusetts, resulted in the first two battles of the Revolutionary War.

George III (1738–1820) · British king during the Revolutionary War.

Hale, Nathan (1755–1776) · A Connecticut Patriot spy, Hale was executed by the British and is famed for his last words: "I only regret that I have but one life to give for my country."

Hamilton, Alexander (1757–1804) · A Continental Army officer and aide to Washington, Hamilton became the first U.S. secretary of the treasury.

Hancock, John (1737–1793) · A revolutionary organizer and president of the Continental Congress, Hancock was the first to sign the Declaration of Independence.

Henry, Patrick (1736–1799) · This Virginia lawyer stirred rebellion with his "give me liberty or give me death" speech (1775).

Jefferson, Thomas (1743–1826) · The principal author of the Declaration of Independence, Jefferson became third president of the United States.

Jones, John Paul (1747–1792) · Born in Scotland, Jones became the greatest American naval hero of the Revolution.

Lafayette, Marquis de (1757–1834) · Lafayette was the most famous of the European officers who helped the United States win the Revolution.

Lee, Henry ("Light Horse Harry") (1756–1818) · A dashing American cavalry commander, he was the father of Civil War general Robert E. Lee.

Lincoln, Benjamin (1733–1810) · Washington chose this Continental Army commander to accept Cornwallis's sword at the Yorktown surrender.

Marion, Francis ("Swamp Fox") (c. 1732–1795) · A wily fighter, Marion was a Patriot military leader in the Carolina wilderness.

North, Frederick (Lord North) (1732–1792) · This British prime minister was responsible for most of the laws and taxes that provoked the American colonists to revolt against King George III.

Revere, Paul (1735–1818) · Silversmith, spy, and courier, Revere earned fame for his "Midnight Ride," which summoned the Minutemen to the Battles of Lexington and Concord (1775).

Rochambeau, Comte de (1725–1807) · This French general shared the Yorktown victory with Washington.

Steuben, Friedrich von (1730–1794) · A Prussian (German) military officer, Steuben helped train the Continental Army.

Washington, George (1732–1799) · Commander in chief of the Continental Army and, later, first president of the United States.